The Natural History Museum
Weird & Wonderful Guides

Going, Going, Gone

Barbara Taylor

PETER BEDRICK BOOKS

Acknowledgments

The publishers would like to thank:

Marwell Zoological Park, National Birds of Prey Centre, Weymouth Sealife Park,
Chelsea Physic Garden, Kings Reptile World, Virginia Cheeseman, Mark O'Shea and the
following staff at The Natural History Museum, London: Barry Bolton, Steve Brooks, Paul Clark, Barry Clarke,
Paul Cornelius, Oliver Crimmen, Peter Forey, Frank Greenaway, Richard Harbord, Daphne Hills, Paul
Hillyard, Paula Jenkins, Carol Levick, Judith Marshall, Colin McCarthy, Angela Milner, Fred Naggs, Cally
Oldershaw, Gordon Paterson, Robert Press, Robert Prys-Jones, Gaden Robinson, Andrew Smith, Chris Stanley,
Frank Steinheimer, John Taylor, Kathie Way, the staff of the EM Unit, Photo Unit, Picture Library and
Publishing Division.

Photography copyright © The Natural History Museum, except the following:
p. 16 tr copyright © BBC Natural History Unit (Nick Garbutt)
p. 7 bl copyright © Natural History Photographic Agency
p. 14 t & b, p. 17 cl copyright © Planet Earth Pictures
p. 18-19 background copyright © Science Photo Library (Renee Lynn)
New photography by Frank Greenaway

The creatures in this book are not reproduced life size, or to scale.

This Americanized Edition of *Going, Going, Gone* originally published in English
in 2001 is published in arrangement with Oxford University Press.

Published in the United States in 2001 by Peter Bedrick Books
A division of NTC/Contemporary Publishing Group, Inc.
4255 West Touhy Avenue, Lincolnwood (Chicago), Illinois 60712-1975 U.S.A.
Text copyright © Barbara Taylor 2000

Printed in China

International Standard Book Number: 0-87226-658-3

10 9 8 7 6 5 4 3 2 1

Library of Congress Cataloging-in-Publication Data
Taylor, Barbara, 1954-
Going, going, gone / Barbara Taylor.
p. cm. — (The Natural History Museum weird and wonderful guides)
ISBN 0-87226-658-3
1. Rare animals—Miscellanea—Juvenile literature. 2. Animals, Fossil—Juvenile literature.
(1. Endangered species—Miscellanea. 2. Rare animals—Miscellanea. 3. Rare plants—Miscellanea. 4. Fossils)
I. Title. II. Series.
QL83 .T28 2001
591.68—dc21   00-56488

Contents

Old and rare

Since life first appeared on Earth about 3,800 million years ago, an incredible variety of creatures has lived, and died out. New living things have gradually taken the place of old ones. When a creature dies out it is gone forever. Many of today's rare species will die out soon if we do not save them.

Nautiluses are related to ammonites, squid and octopuses.

Did You Know ?

The African violet is one of the 20 rarest wild plants in the world today.

Passenger pigeons once nested in colonies of millions of birds. There are none left today.

About 20,000 kinds of plants and animals are in danger of extinction.

Animals looking rather like this have been found preserved as fossils in rocks hundreds of millions of years old. Yet this pearly nautilus lives in today's oceans. It is called a living fossil, because it has not changed over millions of years.

Trilobites lived about 590-250 million years ago. They were the distant relatives of today's shrimps and lobsters. They had many legs and long feelers at the front.

About 300 years ago, people on the island of Mauritius in the Indian Ocean killed the last dodo. Dodos could not fly and were very trusting, so were easy for people to kill and eat. Rats and dogs also ate the dodo's eggs.

A dodo was larger than a wild turkey.

Jaguars are rare because people have hunted them for their fabulous spotty fur. Their rainforest home has also been destroyed.

Fantastic fossils

Looking at fossils is like traveling back in time, to see what plants and animals looked like millions of years ago. Most fossils are the remains of living things buried between layers of rock, and gradually turned to stone. A few special fossils are trapped in amber, natural tar, frozen soil or even mother-of-pearl.

The shape of this fern leaf print is very clear, even though it is hundreds of millions of years old.

These beautiful coiled shells belong to predators, called ammonites, that hunted in the oceans millions of years ago. They had a head and tentacles sticking out of the end of the shell when they were alive.

About 300 million years ago, lots of plants like this fern died and were buried quickly in swampy soil. The plants were pressed together, eventually making the coal we burn today.

Did You Know ?

The largest known ammonite measured 6 feet across.

The oldest fossils are about 3,800 million years old.

The largest piece of transparent amber in the world is 20 inches long.

Millions of years ago, insects were sometimes trapped in the sticky resin that oozed out of the bark of trees. They were preserved if the resin became hard and changed into an orange-yellow substance called amber.

TRUE
or
FALSE

*The hair of dinosaurs
has been found on their fossils?*

*Only about 1 percent of all life on Earth
has been preserved as fossils?*

*Coal is made from
fossil plants?*

?

Answers on page 22

A spider and a cricket are trapped forever inside this piece of polished amber.

9

This fossil fish was swimming about in the sea when huge, long-necked dinosaurs such as *Diplodocus* and *Brachiosaurus* were plodding about on the land.

Can you see the fish fossil in this pearl oyster shell? It is trapped under a shiny layer of mother-of-pearl.

This *Mesturus* fish looks like the scaly fish of today.

Life on Earth

The first living things on Earth, such as algae and corals, developed in the sea. By about 500 million years ago more complex animals, such as fishes, were swimming in the oceans. Life moved onto land about 400 million years ago, with the first land plants and insects. Amphibians and reptiles developed later. Birds and mammals were the last animals to appear.

Anomalocaris had "oars" instead of legs, and "rowed" along.

This strange-looking animal is called *Anomalocaris*. It lived on the sea floor about 530 million years ago. There is nothing like it alive today. Fossils of it were found in the Rocky Mountains in Canada.

Sharks have been around for about 400 million years! The first sharks died out, but the descendants of some groups that lived about 200 million years ago are alive today.

This baby smooth-hound shark has a very bendy body.

Did You Know ?

We humans have been around for only about 400,000 years.

The first sharks lived about 370 million years before the dinosaurs.

Giant sharks 40 feet long swam in the oceans of 15 million years ago.

This is *Megazostrodon*, one of the first mammals of 210 million years ago. They were tiny, secretive, furry animals.

This is a fossil of a frog that lived millions of years ago.

The oldest known bird is called *Archaeopteryx*, which means "ancient wing." It lived about 150 million years ago. It was covered in feathers, but unlike today's birds *Archaeopteryx* had teeth.

The first frogs developed about 240 million years ago, before the dinosaurs. Frogs are amphibians, which live partly on the land and partly in the water.

Incredible dinosaurs

No one has ever seen a living dinosaur. The last ones died out 65 million years ago. But by studying their fossil bones, teeth, droppings and footprints we know what these incredible creatures looked like, what they ate and how fast they moved.

Tyrannosaurus rex

The massive skull was more than one third of the length of the whole animal.

Tyrannosaurus rex had teeth as long as bananas and jaws strong enough to crush bones.

Timid *Hypsilophodon* was one of the fastest dinosaurs. It sprinted along in groups, watching out for danger, as a herd of gazelles might do today.

The name *Triceratops* means three-horned face. *Triceratops* was rather like a huge rhinoceros. It used its horns to fight rivals and enemies, such as *T. rex*.

Pachycephalosaurus has the nickname bonehead, because of its thick, bony crash helmet. This protected its brain during head-butting contests with other males or predators.

vas a reptile with a scaly skin. It weighed more than an African elephant!

Did You Know ?

The word dinosaur means terrible lizard.

Until about 150 years ago, no one knew dinosaurs had ever existed, yet they roamed the Earth for about 160 million years.

Many dinosaurs, like these *Orodromeus*, hatched out of eggs. About 10-30 eggs were laid at a time, in a nest on the ground. These baby plant-eaters could run immediately after hatching.

The bird-like head had a bony crest and a horny beak.

Oviraptor's name means egg thief. It used the sharp spikes in its mouth to break open hard fruits, shellfish - or perhaps dinosaur eggs!

Living fossils

Some animals and plants are almost identical to creatures that lived millions of years ago. These living fossils may be particularly well adapted to their environment, or live in an environment that has hardly changed. Some, such as the Tuatara lizard, live in places where there are no competitors.

The name "coelacanth" means hollow spine.

The curious coelacanth has looked much like this for about 400 million years! Coelacanths were alive when some fishes first crawled out of the water, using fleshy fins to help them move on land.

The Tuatara lived alongside the dinosaurs, and is still around today. Tuataras live on a few small islands off the coast of New Zealand, and come out at night.

Cockroaches today are very similar to those of 300 million years ago. They are very good at surviving.

The pearly nautilus has about 90 long, grasping tentacles to catch prey, such as crabs.

If you had swum in the oceans of 450-500 million years ago, you would have seen a lot of creatures like this pearly nautilus. The oceans are good places to find living fossils, because they change less than land habitats.

The beautiful fan-shaped leaves of the maidenhair, or ginkgo tree, look just like those of fossil ginkgoes that lived about 160 million years ago. Dinosaurs may have nibbled at leaves like these!

Did You Know ?

The coelacanth gives birth to live young instead of laying eggs.

Cockroaches can eat paper, soap, rope and shoelaces.

Rare plants

Tens of thousands of plants in the world are in danger. We are destroying and polluting the places where they live, collecting too many of them and letting farm animals eat them.

Drugs made from the rosy periwinkle have been used to treat some forms of cancer.

The beautiful rosy periwinkle grows in the rapidly disappearing rainforests on the island of Madagascar.

Many rare plants grow on islands. This one comes from the Canary Islands. Island plants may be wiped out by competition from new plants and by animals brought to the islands by people.

Did You Know ?

At least half the world's cycads are threatened with extinction.

When a plant dies out, so do all the animals that depend entirely on it for food and shelter.

The Killarney fern is rare because too many of them have been taken from the wild, and its habitat is polluted.

Cycads have lived on Earth since the days of the dinosaurs, but today they are the world's most threatened plant group. There are only three male plants of this species left in the world.

Pitcher plants like these are rare in the wild because too many of them have been collected for gardens in North America and Europe.

Rare animals

Today, animals are disappearing faster than ever before because of things people do. We build cities, farms and roads on top of their homes so they have nowhere to live. We hunt them for their fur, horns or tusks. And we pollute the world so many animals cannot live in it.

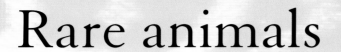

Rhinos are hunted for their horns, which can be sold for a lot of money. This baby white rhino had no horns when he was born! Now, at four months old, he is just growing his front horn.

The spotty fur of the snow leopard is so stunning that people have killed lots of them for fur coats. People and their farm animals have also taken over their mountain home. Only a few thousand are now left in the wild.

18

The okapi is a relative of the giraffe, with a short neck. It is threatened by the destruction of its African rainforest home.

Can you guess why this miniature monkey is called a "lion" tamarin?

Scimitar-horned oryx have probably died out in the wild. Hundreds have been born in zoos though, and some have been sent to live in a national park in Tunisia, North Africa.

19

The rainforest home of the golden lion tamarin has been almost destroyed. There are only about 400 of these tamarins left in the whole world.

Rare treasures

From sparkling crystals and gems to glittering gold and shiny pearls, the Earth's treasures are precious because they are rare and beautiful. They may be rare because they are a special color, or are very hard to find, or because they are an impressive size.

Dazzling emeralds form when the Earth's heat melts substances in the rock.

Perfect emeralds are very expensive because they are rare as well as beautiful. Emerald is a green form of the mineral beryl.

You'd have to be very lucky indeed to find a gold nugget like this! Most gold occurs only as tiny specks in rocks, which have to be added together to make larger pieces. Gold is a soft metal that can easily be bent into shape to make jewelry.

Pearls come in many different colors - even black, green and blue - but all are greatly prized. Natural pearls grow inside the shells of living molluscs, especially oysters and mussels. The mollusc grows a ball of shiny nacre to cover up a grain of sand that gets stuck in its shell.

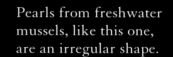

Pearls from freshwater mussels, like this one, are an irregular shape.

TRUE
or
FALSE

*The metal platinum
is worth more than gold?*

It takes about 20 years for a pearl to form?

*A gem's weight was once measured
by comparing it to that of
a carob seed?*

? Answers on page 22

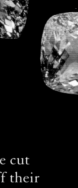

21

Glittering gemstones are cut and polished to show off their beauty. Their surfaces are covered with lots of highly polished, flat surfaces that reflect the light and make them sparkle.

A stunning opal gem, cut from natural rock. Unlike other gems opal has no crystals. It is made of tiny balls of silica, which reflect and scatter light.

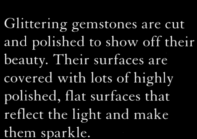

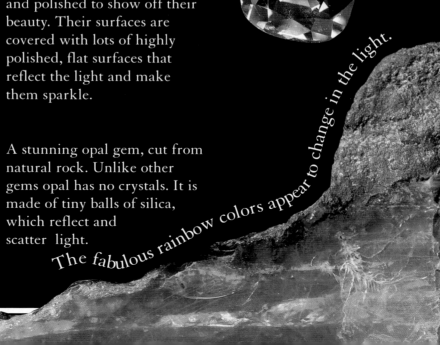

The fabulous rainbow colors appear to change in the light.

Index

22

True or False answers

Old and rare
★ True.
★ True.
★ False, the dodo could not fly.

Fantastic fossils
★ False, dinosaurs were reptiles, not mammals.
  Only mammals have hair.
★ True.
★ True.

Rare treasures
★ True, at the moment.
★ False, it takes about 3-7 years for a large pearl to form.
★ True.